Indian Mutiny: Brief Narrative Of The Defense Of The Arrah Garrison

One Of The Besieged Party

In the interest of creating a more extensive selection of rare historical book reprints, we have chosen to reproduce this title even though it may possibly have occasional imperfections such as missing and blurred pages, missing text, poor pictures, markings, dark backgrounds and other reproduction issues beyond our control. Because this work is culturally important, we have made it available as a part of our commitment to protecting, preserving and promoting the world's literature. Thank you for your understanding.

INDIAN MUTINY

BRIEF

NARRATIVE OF THE DEFENCE

OF THE

ARRAH GARRISON.

WRITTEN BY

ONE OF THE BESIEGED PARTY.

Signed R. V. B.

To accompany Mr. W. Tayler's *Picture of the Attack.*

LONDON:
W. THACKER & Co., 87, NEWGATE STREET.
CALCUTTA: THACKER, SPINK AND CO.
BOMBAY: THACKER & CO.   ALLAHABAD: J. HILL & CO.
1858.

J. & W. RIDER, Printers, 14, Bartholomew Close, London.

DEFENCE OF THE ARRAH GARRISON.

When the 7th, 8th, and 40th Native Infantry Regiments mutinied on the 25th of July at Dinapore, several messengers were despatched to inform the residents at Arrah of the fact.

Arrah is twenty-five miles west of Dinapore, the road being intersected by the river Soane, at about eight miles from Arrah. None of these messengers arrived, the road being already in possession of the rebels, and the first positive evidence of the mutiny received at Arrah was on Sunday, the 26th, when it was ascertained that large numbers of armed men had crossed the Soane, and fired the dwellings &c. of the railway company's officers, who had barely time to escape in boats. During Sunday, the entire body of the rebels crossed the river, and on Monday morning they marched into Arrah, where they were joined by many men on leave, armed mutineers from other districts, who had concealed themselves in the neighbourhood, and a large number of Rajpoots armed with spears and swords, or matchlocks, and headed by Baboo Kooer Sing in person.

It is supposed that there were present, during the greater portion of the siege, three thousand disciplined troops, and about double that number of Kooer Sing's retainers.

On arriving at Arrah, the rebels first went to the jail, released the prisoners, and then took possession of the collectorate, where there was about 85,000 rupees.

This money having been appropriated, a general attack, simultaneous from all sides, was made on the devoted little band, who, with resolute calmness, awaited the onset in a small but strongly barricaded house, fifty feet square.

The besieged consisted of Mr. Littledale, judge; Mr. Combe, collector; Mr. Wake, magistrate; Mr. J. Colvin, assistant; Dr. Hally, civil assistant-surgeon; Mr. Field, sub-deputy opium agent; Mr. Boyle, district engineer to the railway company; Mr. Anderson, Synd A. H. Khan, Messrs. Da Costa, Godfrey, Cock, Tait, Delpeiron, Hayle, and De Souza, with fifty Seikhs and three servants.

The Seikhs were under the immediate command of Mr. Wake, who, having gained their confidence, was ever ready, and proved himself admirably adapted to encourage and control them.

The house in which this little garrison made their stand, was one of two occupied by Mr. Boyle. It had been fortified and provisioned by him for many weeks previously, in anticipation of the disturbances reaching Arrah. Fuel, with water enough for fifty men for a fortnight, a few entrenching tools, some spare ball cartridge, besides gunpowder and lead for making more, had also been provided.

The fortified house consisted of two stories, with a flat roof. To the latter there was a covered means of access from the interior, and on the low parapets sandbags were disposed, to cover the defenders. The lower and upper stories were strongly barricaded, loop-holes being left at convenient distances, and others broken out at the angles of the building where practicable. There was a ten-feet verandah round three sides of the upper story, and one main central room about twenty-four feet square. There was a well-secured postern, or sally-port, on the south side of the building.

Three or four of the best shots were generally on the roof, from whence they had great command of the approaches, and of the roof of the main dwelling-house, which was distant but seventy or eighty yards.

It was at about eight o'clock on Monday morning, 27th of July, that large bodies of the mutinous Sepoys appeared simultaneously on all sides of the enclosure in which the two houses were situated. Skirmishers were thrown rapidly forward, under shelter of trees and shrubs, and advanced, some of them, within fifty yards of the little fort. They were immediately followed by numerous detached parties, who directed volley after volley at the little stronghold, with the evident intention of forcing their way into it, and overwhelming the besieged by their numbers.

The order and discipline that prevailed among the garrison at this trying moment could not be surpassed, and having reserved their fire, according to orders, until the enemy were advancing rapidly in force within from one hundred to two hundred yards of the fort, they now opened so hot and well-directed a fire that many of the mutineers being killed or wounded, the others halted, staggered by the unexpected vigour of the defenders, and after a few moments' hesitation, broke from companies into small groups, and made quickly for the cover of the large trees that studded the compound, while the main body of the rebels getting into, on, and under cover of the main dwelling-house, poured a tremendous fire of musketry in through every opening of the fortification. The cover of the latter was so admirably adapted for the convenience and protection of the defenders, that they were enabled to keep up a steady fire wherever and whenever the enemy showed themselves. This spirited and exciting state of things continued without intermission until midday, with palpable loss to the enemy, who abandoned several of their wounded men in the open air, where they lingered, one of them for two days, until death terminated their miserable career.

About noon, the main body of the enemy drew off, doubtless for food, and to concert measures for further operations, leaving numerous sharpshooters on every side, whose fire was galling and incessant. Between three and four in the afternoon an attack similar, but not so well sustained as that of the morning, was made, and the insurgents were again driven off by the determined and steady fire of the besieged. Soon after sunset, there was a cessation of hostilities, and from the cover of one of the large trees a loud voice was heard addressing the Seikhs, offering them large bribes, and holding out every inducement that could be supposed to weigh with them, if they would turn traitors and join the rebels. All offers were rejected with scorn; and, although repeated daily during the remainder of the week, no answers, after the first day, were vouchsafed, except from the carbines and rifles of the besieged.

On the morning of the 28th, large piles of straw, bamboos, wood, fuel, and other inflammable material, on which were heaped quantities of chilies, were found to have been carried, during the night, to within a short distance of the little fort, and being soon after fired, dense volumes of acrid smoke rolled towards the besieged, and for a short time threatened to suffocate them. This, however, was not to be, for as the fire burned the wind freshened, the smoke became less annoying, and as the flames died away, there was seen on the borders of the smoking embers the half-charred body of one of the insurgents, who had been shot through the portable cover under which he had approached. Soon after this it was evident that new tactics were to be adopted, and right and left of the large dwelling-house could be seen a growing pile of furniture, tossed out in heaps, under cover of which two small guns were got into a position, and their fire at once directed on the besieged. The first discharges were accompanied by loud shouts of anticipated triumph, which the noble little garrison heard in resolute silence. This was succeeded shortly by some degree of amusement, when it was ascertained that the contents of the cannon which came rattling through the defences consisted chiefly of heavy brass castors, torn by the mutineers from pianos, easy chairs, and couches, pending a supply of ammunition more suited to batter down the walls of the little fort. This was soon brought, and for nearly six days and nights, with occasional intervals, a cannonade was kept up from these guns, shifted now to the roof of the large dwelling-house, again to the east, and afterwards to the south of the fort, where, from the cover of ditch and garden wall, the enemy were sheltered from the marksmen of the besieged.

The heavier of the guns threw but four-pound shot, which proved insufficient to breach the walls, although portions of the building had become shaken from repeated discharges taking effect about the same place.

Up to the morning of the 29th, one only of the garrison, a Seikh, was dangerously wounded. On this day, three-quarters of a mile distant, some thousands, a mixed and motley force, could be seen, drawn up and harangued by Kooer Sing, who, it was afterwards ascertained, taunted the Sepoys especially at being so long kept at bay by a mere handful of Seikhs and Christians.

About half-past eleven P.M. of the 29th, high above the reports of the guns and the occasional discharge of small arms, were suddenly heard heavy and rolling volleys of musketry, apparently not a mile away. Dropping shots then followed, and again occasional volleys, which appeared to grow fainter, and indicate that a relieving force from the direction of Dinapore had been defeated, and obliged to retire with loss. This conjecture proved but too true, for a little before dawn on the 30th, one of the defeated force, a wounded Seikh, succeeded in crawling past the rebel sentries, and reaching the little fortress, where he was welcomed with mingled feelings of excitement and sorrow, when it was ascertained that a detachment from Dinapore of four hundred and fifty men, of whom he was one, fell into an ambuscade when within a mile of the fort, and were driven back wholly disorganized, with heavy loss. Relief was now more distant than ever, but hope and trust, and reliance on Providence and on each other, cheered and supported the little band of heroes.

It was feared that water would run short, and the well, which had been begun the previous evening through the lower story, was completed at noon to a depth of about eighteen feet, when a plentiful supply of good water was reached, and the joyful event was hailed by all, the brave Seikhs especially, as a good omen. The earth taken from the well was invaluable for, and materially aided in, strengthening and repairing shattered defences.

It was now found that ball cartridge was running short, some of the Seikhs being reduced to five rounds a man; to supply this deficiency numbers of bullets were run, and during that and the succeeding day, some thousand rounds of ball cartridge were made. Caps, too, ran short, but a few boxes of the larger size for the European guns were tried, and made to answer.

All were now full of confidence; but the want of animal food being felt, a sally was made in the dusk of the evening, and four sheep brought in, which had been confined in an adjoining enclosure. The stock of provisions was examined, and enough was found to last for a fortnight.

On this night, that of the 30th, and the succeeding, larger numbers of men and elephants than usual were collected behind the large house, which afforded effectual shelter to the enemy from the besieged. It was supposed an attempt would be made to carry the little fort by storm, and every precaution possible was made by the garrison, who, knowing that death by cruel torture awaited all who might fall into the hands of the rebels, were prepared to sell their lives as dearly as possible. The Seikhs were armed with carbines and swords; most of the Europeans and East Indians, besides two double guns, or a gun and a rifle, had a revolver, with a heavy hogspear, to repel stormers. Alarms were frequent throughout these nights, and the garrison were harassed by repeated calls from the enemy for the assembly and assault. No direct night attack, however, took place, the rebels confining themselves to repeated discharges from the small cannon and musketry.

The *ping* of the rifle bullet was now too distinctly heard, many of the enemy having (as was afterwards ascertained) supplied themselves with the Enfield rifles and ammunition, which had belonged to men of the 37th Queen's, who had formed a part of the relieving force from Dinapore.

It was at this time that it was ascertained, beyond a doubt, that the enemy were driving a mine from some outhouses not thirty yards distant. The direction was determined, a countermine was commenced, and in an incredibly short time was pushed forward sufficiently to command and baffle the enemy's operations.

About the middle of the week the effluvia which arose from the carcases of four horses shot by the mutineers, within twenty yards of the fort, added to that of one or two dead bodies, also lying near, became at times almost intolerable; but the wind freshening and slightly changing, in some degree latterly relieved the besieged. Birds of prey and jackals had picked the bones of all those who were killed at a distance, but the almost incessant fire from and around the little fort, kept them at this time more distant visitors than the garrison could have wished.

On Sunday, the 2nd of August, although a cannonade and occasional fire of musketry was kept up all day, there were but few assailants to be seen, though signs of much excitement were visible towards the town, whence crowds of people were hurrying with carts, elephants, camels, and horses, laden with plunder.

Throughout the day, faintly and at intervals, were heard the distant reports of cannon to the westward. Soon after sunset the last of the enemy disappeared, and it was ascertained that the siege was raised. Caution, however, was still necessary, and before midnight the enemy's guns had been secured and dragged within the fort, together with a quantity of powder which had been provided for the mine.

That night peaceful and quiet watches were passed, and the next morning, Monday, the 3rd of August, the victorious little garrison had the joy of welcoming the noble band of 230 men, who, with three guns, under the gallant Eyre, had marched from Buxan, and, at some miles from Arrah, on the previous day, encountered and signally defeated the main body of the mutineers.

Subsequent operations, with the united forces further strengthened, were undertaken with brilliant results; but here ended the siege, one of the most remarkable—perhaps the most extraordinary and signal instance of house defence on record, during which some sixty-seven men repulsed the continued and desperate attacks of one hundred times their number of foes, at once cunning, cruel, and implacable.

The defence of Arrah will long be remembered in Indian history, and long will the little garrison be remembered for the sustained courage, the stern resolution, fertility of resource, and unyielding energy so eminently displayed. The principal events of this remarkable week at Arrah are here described, but of minor ones there are none that mark the calm and settled purpose of the besieged more than the fact of a diary having been inscribed daily on the wall, that it at least might tell the tale, should none of them be left to do so.

R. V. B.

The following is communicated from H. C. WAKE, Esq., Magistrate of Shahabad, to W. TAYLER, Esq., Commissioner of the Patna Division.

"SIR,—I have the honour to forward, for the information of His Honour the Lieutenant-Governor, the following narrative of our extraordinary defence and providential escape. On the evening of Saturday, July the 25th, I received an express from Dinapore, warning us that a disturbance was apprehended on that day, but giving us no other information. On the morning of July the 26th, a Sowar, whom I had posted at Koelwar Ghat, on the Soane, came in and reported that numbers of Sepoys had crossed, and that more were crossing.

"I found that Mr. Palin, the railway engineer stationed at Koelwar, had contented himself with sending over for the boats to the Arrah side the night before, but when leaving, had failed to destroy them, as he had promised to do. The police, I imagine, bolted at the first alarm.

"All efforts to ascertain the amount of the force of the rebels were unavailing, and the police left the city on Sunday the 26th. Thinking it highly unadvisable to abandon the station when the rebels might be few, and having fifty Seikhs on the spot, and finding the rest of the officers of the station of the same opinion, and the few residents in the district who had come in to us willing to remain, we, on the night of Sunday the 26th, went into a small bungalow, previously fortified as much as possible by Mr. Boyle, the district engineer of the railway company.

"Our force consisted of one Jemadar, two Havildars, two Naicks, forty-five Privates, a bhistee and cook of Captain Rattray's Seikh

Police Battalion; Mr. Littledale, judge; Mr. Combe, officiating collector; Mr. Wake, magistrate; Mr. Colvin, assistant; Dr. Hally, civil assistant-surgeon; Mr. Field, sub-deputy opium agent; Mr. Anderson, his assistant; Mr. Boyle, district engineer to the railway company; Synd Azumudeen Hossein, deputy collector; Mr. Da Costa, moonsiff; Mr. Godfrey, schoolmaster; Mr. Cock, officiating head clerk of the Collectorate; Mr. Tait, secretary to Mr. Boyle; Messrs. Delpeiron and Hayle, railway inspectors, and Mr. De Souza.

"We had enough atta and grain for some days of short allowance, and a good deal of water for ourselves; but owing to the shortness of our notice, nothing but the barest necessities could be brought in, and the Seikhs had only a few days' water, but as we expected the rebels to be followed up immediately, we had not much anxiety on that score.

"On Monday, the 27th July, about 8 a. m.,

the insurgent Sepoys, the whole of the 7th, 8th, and 46th Native Infantry, arrived in the station, and having first released the prisoners, rushed to the Collectorate, where they were at once joined by the Nujeebs, and looted the treasure, amounting to 85,000 rupees. This did not take long, and they then charged our bungalow from every side, but being met with a steady and well-directed fire, they changed their tactics, and hiding behind the trees with which the compound is filled, and occupying the outhouses, and Mr. Boyle's residence, which was unfortunately within sixty yards of our fortification, they kept up an incessant and galling fire on us during the whole day. They were joined by numbers of Kooer Sing's men, and the Sepoys repeatedly declared that they were acting under his express orders; and after a short time he was seen on the parade, and remained during the siege. Every endeavour was made by the rebels to induce the Seikhs to abandon us; heavy bribes were offered to them, and their own countrymen employed as mediators. They treated every offer with derision, showing perfect obedience and discipline.

"On the 28th two small cannons were brought to play upon our bungalow, one throwing 4-lb. shot, and these were daily shifted to what the rebels thought to be our weakest spots; finally the largest was placed on the roof of Mr. Boyle's dwelling-house, completely commanding the inside of our bungalow, and the smaller behind it at a distance of twenty yards. Nothing but cowardice, want of unanimity, and only the ignorance of our enemies prevented our fortification being brought down about our ears.

"During the entire siege, which lasted seven days, every possible stratagem was practised against us. The cannons were fired as frequently as they could prepare shot, with which they were at first unprovided, and incessant assaults were made upon the bungalow. Not only did our Seikhs behave with perfect coolness and patience, but their untiring labour met and prevented every threatened disaster. Water began to run short; a well, eighteen feet by four, was dug in less than twelve hours. The rebels raised a barricade on the top of the opposite house; our own grew in the same proportion. A shot shook a weak place in our defence; the place was made twice as strong as before. We began to feel the want of animal food, and short allowance of grain; a sally was made at night, and four sheep brought in; and, finally, when we ascertained, beyond a doubt, that the enemy were undermining us, a countermine was quickly dug.

"On the 30th, the troops sent to our relief from Dinapore were attacked and beaten back, close to the entrance of the town. On the next day the rebels returned, and telling us that they had annihilated our relief, offered the Seikhs, and the women and children (of whom there were none with us) their lives and liberty if they would give up the Government officers.

"August the 1st, we were all offered our lives, and leave to go to Calcutta, if we should give up our arms. On the 2nd, the greater part of the Sepoys went out to meet Major Eyre's field force, and on their being soundly thrashed, the rest of them deserted the station, and that night we went out and found their mine had reached our foundations, and a canvass tube filled with gunpowder was lying handy to blow us up; in which, however, I do not think that they would have succeeded, as their powder was bad, and another stroke of their pickaxe would have broken into our countermine. We also brought in the one gun which they had left on the top of the opposite house.

"During the whole siege, only one man, a Seikh, was severely wounded, though two or three got scratches and blows from splinters and bricks. Every one in our garrison behaved well, but I should be neglecting a duty did I omit to mention specially Mr. Boyle, to whose engineering skill and untiring exertions we in a great measure owe our preservation; and Mr. Colvin, who rendered the most valuable assistance, and who rested neither night nor day, and took on himself far more than his share of every disagreeable duty. In conclusion, I most earnestly beg that his Honour the Lieutenant-Governor, will signally reward the whole of our gallant little detachment of Seikhs, whose service and fidelity cannot be overrated. The Jemadar should at once be made a Subadar, and many of the rest are fit for promotion, and when required I will submit a list with detail.

"I have, &c.,

(Signed) "H. C. WAKE, *Magistrate.*"

THE LEADING INDIAN QUARTERLY.
Price Rs. 5,

THE CALCUTTA REVIEW. The CALCUTTA REVIEW, commenced in 1843, has long received the support of the most accomplished writers on every subject of interest connected with Anglo-India, and its largely increasing circulation proves the high estimation in which it is now held.

FOR FREEMASONS.

THE INDIAN FREEMASONS' MAGAZINE, embracing every Subject relative to the Craft in India, with Intelligence of the Lodge Meetings, Royal Arch Chapters, &c., &c. Published Monthly, price Rs. 16 per annum.

Octavo, 5s.,

MAJOR C. F. TROWER'S CONFORMATION, MANAGEMENT, and USE of the IRREGULAR CAVALRY of INDIA.

In 2 vols., post 8vo., price 18s.,

A VOLUNTEER'S SCRAMBLE THROUGH SCINDE, the PUNJAUB, HINDOSTAN, and the HIMALAYAH MOUNTAINS. By Lieut. HUGO JAMES, Bengal Army.

Just Published, price Rs. 9,

BRIGADIER SYDNEY COTTON'S PESHAWUR FIELD EXERCISES, Demy 8vo., with 25 Diagrams executed at the Surveyor-General's Office: Consisting of Two Field Days—Horse and Foot Artillery; Four Field Days—Horse Artillery and Cavalry; Two Field Days—Infantry and Light Field Batteries; Two Field Days—Three Arms combined. With diagrams and memoranda illustrative and explanatory of the various manœuvres. By BRIGADIER SYDNEY COTTON, Commanding Peshawur Field Forces.

MR. H. W. TORRENS' REMARKS on the SCOPE and USES of MILITARY LITERATURE and HISTORY. Reduced in price from Rs. 8 to 5.

London: W. THACKER & Co., 87, Newgate Street.
Calcutta: THACKER, SPINK, & Co.; Bombay: THACKER & Co.

Just Published, price 2s.,

A PERSONAL JOURNAL of the SIEGE of LUCKNOW. By Major R. P. ANDERSON, 25th Regt. N.I., commanding an Outpost, author of the "Translation of the Gool-i-Bakawli," &c., &c.; edited, with a Preface and Introduction, by T. CARNEGY ANDERSON, Lieut. 12th Regt. N.I.

Lately Published, price, plain, 20s. coloured, 30s.

CALCUTTA FRUITS. A LITHOGRAPH from the large Oil Painting by Lieut.-Col. H. B. HENDERSON (Bengal Army), which attracted so much attention when exhibited at the Crystal Palace. The copy has been most successfully executed by French Artists, and will form an interesting memento to all who are in any way connected with India. The subject consists of a pile of Calcutta Fruits, around which are grouped characters illustrative of the following extract from a "Journal in Calcutta:"—"Our pretty Ayah is constantly taking our child among the servants. The child's bearer is very jealous at this, and hints that the attraction is the Consumah."

PRINCE GHOLAM MOHAMMED'S HISTORY OF HYDER ALI AND TIPPOO SULTAUN.

Now ready, in royal 8vo, handsomely bound, price 14s.,

THE HISTORY of HYDER SHAH, alias HYDER ALI KHAN BAHADUR, and of his Son, TIPPOO SULTAUN. Revised and Corrected by his Highness Prince Gholam Mohammed, the only surviving Son of Tippoo Sultaun. This work affords an interesting view of Indian Politics and Warfare, as related by Native Historians

---

Four Vols., royal 8vo., sewed, £4 4s.,

THE ALIF LAILA; or, ARABIAN NIGHTS ENTERTAINMENTS, in the Original Arabic. Edited by the late Sir W. H. MACNAGHTEN.

12mo., 6s.,

DR. MORRISON'S ENGLISH and CHINESE VOCABULARY.

London: W. THACKER & Co., 87, Newgate Street.
Calcutta: THACKER, SPINK, & Co. Bombay: THACKER & Co.

THE CHEAPEST AND BEST NEWSPAPER PUBLISHED IN LONDON
FOR DESPATCH TO INDIA AND THE EAST.

Thirty-two pages, with Supplements when necessary,
Price 5d.,

THACKER'S OVERLAND NEWS,

FOR INDIA AND THE COLONIES.

This Newspaper, unsurpassed for cheapness and excellence, is published on the afternoons of the 2nd, 9th, 17th, and 25th of each month, in time for despatch to India and China, *via* Marseilles.

The Intelligence in THACKER'S OVERLAND NEWS is brought down to the latest possible moment, so as to place the Indian public in possession of all important information to within a few hours of the departure of the Mail.

It presents a comprehensive and perfect view of British and Foreign affairs, with special reference to those subjects in any way interesting to residents in India, or those at home having connections there. The various departments are so arranged, and the intelligence analysed, as to form a weekly register of permanent interest and value, which subscribers will be glad to preserve.

The weekly issue of THACKER'S OVERLAND NEWS renders it as eligible a newspaper for Anglo-Indians resident at home as abroad.

Families should send it as a present to their friends abroad.

Parties proceeding to India or China should not fail to order a year's subscription.

SUBSCRIPTION, including Marseilles Postage,
Per Year......... Rs.16, payable in advance.

Subscriptions are received, and the Paper forwarded to all parts of the World, by

W. THACKER & Co., 87, Newgate Street, London.
Calcutta: THACKER, SPINK, & Co. Bombay: THACKER & Co.;
Allahabad: J. HILL & Co.;
also, E. MARLBOROUGH & Co., Ave Maria Lane, London;
and all News Agents in England and India.

Printed by Libri Plureos GmbH in Hamburg,
Germany